C000095146

The Master

&

The Maid

...Ways To Fostering A Healthy Relationship

Ruth Osasu Omoregie

The Master and The Maid

Copyright: © 2012 Ruth Osasu Omoregie

Phone: +353 (0) 86 397 8440
Email: ruthgfm@yahoo.co.uk

ISBN: 978-0-9564927-6-0

Published by:
Lacepoint Publishing
Website: www.lacepoint.ie
Email: services@lacepoint.ie
Tel: +353 1 442 8309

All Scripture, unless otherwise stated, are taken from the New King James Version of the Bible. Copyright 1979, 1980, 1982, 1990, Thomas Nelson Inc.

Printed in the Republic of Ireland.

Dedication

I dedicate this book to God my creator, to the Lord Jesus Christ for the ransom He paid for my salvation and to the Holy Spirit my great and reliable comforter, to whom all secrets belong to and the one that empowers one for greatness.

I also dedicate this book to all workers in service most especially in the house of God. God Almighty will encourage and reward you all.

Acknowledgement

My first appreciation goes to Almighty God the father for creating me, to God the son for the gift of abundant life and to the Holy Spirit for His enabling grace, mercy and inspiration to write this book.

I am sincerely grateful to my dearest husband, Nosakhare Omoregie who gave me the opportunity to serve in the ministry and also provided a conducive environment which a project of this nature demands and my loving children, for their wonderful support, deep understanding and all round encouragement. I will not have been able to make much progress today without your understanding considering the nature of my job and the time involved. God will continue to pour His showers of blessings on you all.

A sincere appreciation goes to my biological parents Mr. Michael & Deaconess Roseline Omorotionmwan that laid the foundation for my spiritual and educational pursuit. You gave me the best of education not because you are wealthy but you believe that education is the best legacy that a parent can leave for a child. I am very grateful to you, Dad & Mum. May you continue to enjoy the fruits of your labour.

Also, my appreciation goes to my spiritual father, Pastor John Olusoga Fasan who initiated the idea and pushed me on to actualise this dream. Thanks for giving me the opportunity to serve in the ministry under your leadership and supervision. My work with you has broadened my dreams and aspirations in life. It is difficult for anyone in your company not to have a sense of direction or purpose. You did not allow my position to hinder the utilisation of my God given potentials. I am very grateful. My appreciation also goes to my spiritual mother, Pastor Helen Fasan. This book is a product of your trust and believe in me. Thanks for being there.

I am grateful to all my siblings Deaconess Eunice O. Abu, Mrs Susan O. Omofoma, Engr. (Deac.) Jude O. Omorotionmwan, Deaconess Maria A. Afam and Mrs Stephanie O. Edosomwan for all your prayers and encouragement and support. I am most grateful to

Deaconess Eunice Abu who has been my spiritual role model from childhood for creating time out of her tight schedule to proof read this work.

I am very grateful to my in-law, my big brother in the Lord and a very good friend Pastor Osarumen Obayagbonna for his moral support in ensuring I completed this book without much worries. Your encouragement in words and in kind can never be forgotten.

My appreciation goes to my mentor, intercessor and a dear God mother, Pastor Funmi Ogunsanwo for her encouragement and prayers for the past nine years. Mum, you have been a pillar of support to my family and I and it is my prayer that the ministry committed into your hands by the almighty God will grow from strength to strength in Jesus name, Amen.

My appreciation also goes to my friend and colleague Mrs. Tomike Fadojutimi for her encouragement and love expressed towards me. God almighty will always remember you and to all Ministers and members of

Gospel Faith Mission International for their encouragement. God will continue to shower His blessings on you all.

Finally, I wish to express my appreciation to my friend and publisher of this book Clem Roberts for the time taken to ensure that the production is of a good quality. Thank you very much Sir.

TABLE OF CONTENT

Foreword

This book is an inspirational and heart to heart word of wisdom that we need. The principles of this book apply to employees and employers in every age, whether in the home, in the business, church or corporate institution. The principles in this book will work, you don't have to be gifted or exceptionally bright to employ this truth in your life as a Master or Maid but you must be willing.

Ruth, by the grace of God was able to reveal the deepest need of a Master and the expectation of the Maid. Most of the qualities of maid in this book are unique qualities in her life that has made her my unique assistant in the Ministry. She is a person you can rely on and her passion for the work makes a big difference.

1 Cor.4:2 Moreover it is required in stewards that a man be found faithful. There is no respect of person with God. Everyone is going to get exactly what he has laboured for upon this earth regardless of his profession, wealth, position and poverty. A Christian either the Master or the Maid is to work with the fear of God in their heart. Both are to discharge their responsibilities with singleness of heart, in sincerity and without any pretence or hypocrisy or slack.

Those who find themselves in the category of Maid, I urge you not to work with eyes service as a man's pleaser but to work diligently as though your boss is the Lord Jesus Christ and not man. The employer expects at least two things – Diligence and Loyalty. The charge to the employer is the same - be diligent in your management and in your loyalty to the people under you, demonstrating your loyalty with fair wages and job security. Every step should be taken to teach and train even the most unproductive staff and guard against unwarranted threats for they too have a Master in heaven.

Every church leader, Chief executive and Staff should read this book. I am completely unreserved in recommending her book because I know her very well. God Bless You.

Shalom.

Pastor John O Fasan

One

INTRODUCTION

The master and the maid is a book I decided to put together to be a blessing to the people rendering services to other people at some stage in their lives. I decided to write this book to give a clear exposition of the responsibilities, pains and rewards of being a maid. Also to make masters understand that there are thoughts going on in the hearts of maids and these include fear, expectations of rewards, struggles of the present and anxieties about the future and moreover to reveal some hidden hurts that the maid find difficult to express most especially those serving in the body of Christ.

There are so many mysteries hidden inside a maid. Have you sometimes wonder how maids can handle multiple tasks within a short time? How about being submissive amidst hurts? How about the desire to go on without expecting anything in return? How about not willing to give up amidst difficult situation and circumstance? How about even when people around you cannot comprehend the reason why you are still hanging on despite the unappealing nature of your work circumstance? These are all mysteries. A maid that discovers these mysteries is the one that is able to fulfil destiny because being a maid in the vineyard of God is not slavery. It is a calling and to every call, there is an allocation of grace attached to it. A maid that has an insight of her calling will discover God's purpose for serving. Such a maid in that position is divinely assigned. These are maids sent by God to serve but on the contrary, the maids that are unable to discover this, ends up being destructive. As a female, the day you get married, you become a wife and a maid.

There are two categories of a maid and they fall into either category A (a maid on a godly mission) or category B (a maid on an evil mission). Ruth in the book of Ruth in the Holy Bible is an example of a category A maid. She was a wife and a maid and these qualities and understanding helped her to fulfil purpose and her name was written in the annals of the Holy Bible. She became an epitome of a godly woman.

Ruth 3:9 "And he said, "Who are you?" So she answered, "I am Ruth, your maidservant. Take your maidservant under your wing, for you are a close relative."

Delilah is a category B maid. Delilah on the other hand was a maid on an evil mission. She was a destructive maid and she used her position to destroy Samson. *Judges 16 (NKJV) Afterward it happened that he loved a woman in the Valley of Sorek, whose name was Delilah. 5 And the lords of the Philistines came up to her and said to her, "Entice him, and find out where his great strength lies, and by what means we may overpower him, that we may bind him to afflict him; and every one of us will give you eleven hundred pieces of silver."6 So Delilah said to Samson, "Please tell me* where your great strength lies, and with what you may be bound to afflict you." 16 And it came to pass, when she pestered him daily with her words and pressed him, so that his soul was vexed to death, 17 that he told her all his heart, and said to her, "No razor has ever come upon my head, for I have been a Nazirite to God from my mother's womb. If I am shaven, then my strength will leave me, and I shall become weak, and be like any other man." 18 When Delilah saw that he had told her all his heart, she sent and called for the lords of the Philistines, saying, "Come up once more, for he has told me all his heart." So the lords of the Philistines came up to her and brought the money in their hand. 19 Then she lulled him to sleep on her knees, and called for a man and had him shave off the seven locks of his head. Then she began to torment him, and his strength left him. 20 And she said, "The Philistines are upon you, Samson!" So he awoke from his sleep, and said, "I will go out as before, at other times, and shake myself free!" But he did not know that the Lord had departed from him. 21 Then the Philistines took him and put out his eyes, and brought him down to Gaza. They bound him with bronze fetters, and he became a grinder in the prison. 22 However, the hair of his head began to grow again after it had been shaven.

Though Samson was able to fulfil purpose but this was by God's divine intervention. Samson went through pain before fulfilling destiny. He lost his sight, his strength, his liberty, his credibility and his usefulness. Probably, he would have done more for God but Delilah cut short his destiny. Samson died a prisoner of the Philistines. Some masters have lost their sight spiritually by reason of having a destructive maid. A master who has lost his spiritual sight has also lost his strength, liberty, credibility and usefulness.

It is of necessity you identify your position based on the above illustration. Are you a maid like "Ruth" or "Delilah"? I pray that as I receive inspirations to put these materials together, it will indeed be a blessing to those in service and those intending to go into service and to those being served. The Holy Spirit will give you more understanding as you read through this book. God bless you.

Two

WHO IS A MASTER AND WHO IS A MAID?

A Master is someone placed over somebody or a group of people in the place of service. He is a ruler of a group of people. He is meant to be served. The wife of a master is called a mistress. She also can as well be lord over someone or a group of people. Services are rendered to a master/mistress and those that rendered such services are known as servants. In feminine context, they are called maids. But in this book the main focus is on master/maid relationship but if you fall within a different category based on gender, the Holy Spirit will grant you a deeper understanding in the name of Jesus; Amen.

A maid is a female assigned to serve. She is also called a maidservant or a woman servant. She is a complex creature made by God. There are some features that God did not create in a man but He decided to feature them in a woman. These are the breasts and the womb. These are very important features for help or destruction in the execution of her task. It was after the creation of woman that God rested. God rested because He was satisfied with the product of His work and not because He was tired.

As a relationship conscious being, a woman understands the boundaries of any relationship she finds herself except she is a woman of deceit. As a maid in service, it is important to take time to understand your master, his family and his environment. As you understand these, it is equally important you know your boundaries. Some boundaries are spiritually, physically and morally set. The Master may also set some boundaries and it is of importance you should also have personal boundaries. Along the line, the Master may decide to remove some boundaries set by him by reason of trust and growth in your relationship. But spiritual boundaries are permanent and should not be toiled with. A MASTER WILL ALWAYS REMAIN A MASTER AS LONG AS HE IS BEING SERVED BY YOU. Never become too familiar and begin to destroy God's laid down rules of Master and servant relationship. If you do, you may never enjoy the blessing. Such actions usually end up in shame and disgrace.

The capacity of a Master's prosperity (spiritual and financial) is measured by the number of servants he has. In the bible, we will observe that the wealth of a master is determined by the number of maidservants he has.

Genesis 24:35, *"The LORD has blessed my master abundantly, and he has become wealthy. He has given him sheep and cattle, silver and gold, menservants and maidservants, and camels and donkeys."* (NIV)

Genesis 26:13-14, *"The man began to prosper, and continued prospering until he became very prosperous;* [14] *for he had possessions of flocks and possessions of herds and a great number of servants. So the Philistines envied him."*

Genesis 30:43, "Thus the man became exceedingly prosperous, and had large flocks, female and male servants, and camels and donkeys."

It is required of the servants (menservants or maidservants) to assist in the successful daily operation of the master's business or farmland to ensure high profits or increase in harvest, and also to work in his home and help to meet the needs of his wives and children. The master's expectations from the maidservant are a lot especially when she is a hard worker.

Matthew 24:45, "Who then is a faithful and wise servant, whom his master made ruler over his household, to give them food in due season? 46 Blessed is that servant whom his master, when he comes, will find so doing."

A maid could be hired or purchased. A hired maidservant will receive freedom after the period of hire has elapsed. Then, she is free. But the maidservant that has been purchased is required to serve her master till she dies or until he decides otherwise.

Leviticus 25:39 – 55, "And if one of your brethren who dwells by you becomes poor, and sells himself to you, you shall not compel him to serve as a slave. [40] As a hired servant and a sojourner he shall be with you, and shall serve you until the Year of Jubilee. [41] And then he shall depart from you – he and his children with him – and shall return to his own family. He shall return to the possession of his fathers. [42] For they are My servants, whom I brought out of the land of Egypt; they shall not be sold as slaves. [43] You shall not rule over him with rigor, but you shall fear your God. [44] And as for your male and female slaves whom you may have – from the nations that are around you, from them you may buy male and female slaves. [45] Moreover you may buy the children of the strangers who dwell among you, and their families who are with you, which they beget in your land; and they shall become your property. [46] And you may take them as an inheritance for your children after you, to inherit them as a possession; they shall be your permanent slaves. But regarding your brethren, the children of Israel, you shall not rule over one another with rigor. [47]Now if a sojourner or stranger close to you becomes rich, and one of your brethren who dwells by him becomes poor, and sells himself to the stranger or sojourner close to you, or to a member of the stranger's family, [48] after he is sold he may be redeemed again. One of his brothers may redeem him; [49] or his uncle or his uncle's son may redeem him; or anyone who is near of kin to him in his family may redeem him; or if he is able he may redeem himself. [50] Thus he shall reckon with him who bought him: The price of his release shall be according to the number of years, from the year that he was sold to him until the Year of Jubilee; it shall be according to the time of a hired servant for him. [51] If there are still many years remaining, according to them he shall repay the price of his redemption from the money with which he was bought. [52] And if there remain but a few years until the Year of Jubilee, then he shall reckon with him, and according to his years he shall repay him the price of his redemption. [53] He shall be with him as a yearly hired servant, and he shall not rule with rigor over him in your sight. [54] And if he is not redeemed in these years, then he shall be released in the Year of Jubilee — he and his children with him. [55] For the children of Israel are servants to Me; they are My servants whom I brought out of the land of Egypt: I am the LORD your God."

It is required of a maid to be obedient to her master. I will not classify obedience as a quality but a requirement. There is no other perfect word to replace this. The bible requires that a servant should be obedient.

Ephesians 6:5-8, "Bondservants, be obedient to those who are your masters according to the flesh, with fear and trembling, in sincerity of heart, as to Christ; 6 not with eye service, as men-pleasers, but as bondservants of Christ, doing the will of God from the heart, 7 with goodwill doing service, as to the Lord, and not to men, 8 knowing that whatever good anyone does, he will receive the same from the Lord, whether he is a slave or free".

Colossians 3:22-25, "Bondservants, obey in all things your masters according to the flesh, not with eye service, as men-pleasers, but in sincerity of heart, fearing God. 23 And whatever you do, do it heartily, as to the Lord and not to men, 24 knowing that from the Lord you will receive the reward of the inheritance; for you serve the Lord Christ. 25 But he who does wrong will be repaid for what he has done, and there is no partiality."

1Peter 2:18- 19, "Servants, be submissive to your masters with all fear, not only to the good and gentle, but also to the harsh. 19 For this is commendable, if because of conscience toward God one endures grief, suffering wrongfully."

As a maid, you are required to obey your master even when it may not be convenient to do so. It is impossible to serve well without obedience. This type of obedience is godly and it's free from hypocrisy. It is total. Anything less of total obedience is partial obedience and partial obedience equals total disobedience and this has grievous consequences. There is reward for both obedience and disobedience here on earth and after life. The afterlife reward for obedience is eternal life with our Lord Jesus while disobedience is eternal condemnation to hell.

Total obedience does not demand that you obey when commanded to do the wrong thing especially getting involve with unfruitful works of darkness such as adultery, stealing, murder, telling lies and so on. As a child of God who has knowledge that these are sinful acts, you should not be involved in such acts.

Ephesian 5:8 - 12 For you were once darkness, but now you are light in the Lord. Walk as children of light 9 (for the fruit of the Spirit is in all goodness, righteousness, and truth), 10 finding out what is acceptable to the Lord. 11 And have no fellowship with the unfruitful works of darkness, but rather expose them. 12 For it is shameful even to speak of those things which are done by them in secret.

When you obey in this regard, you will become a partaker of such ungodly act. God does not support such an action and as you know, everyone will stand independently before God on the last day to give an account for the life lived on earth.

As I receive inspiration to put these materials and information together, my focus will be on master and maid relationship in the church and these are the maids that work with men of God on permanent or temporal basis. They are paid staff and volunteers. These are: Secretaries, Administrators, Pastoral Care Staff, Personal Assistants, Protocol officers, Hospitality workers, Ministerial Welfare Team, Drivers, Cooks or anyone whose main responsibility is to serve the master. It is my prayer that this book will be an instrument of blessing to you and your ministry.

Three

QUALITIES OF A MAID

The qualities of a maid are as follows:

Must be decent.

Must be humble and respectful.

Must be quiet

Must be gentle

Must be hospitable

Must be energetic

Must possess initiative

Must be loyal

Must be trustworthy

Must be courteous

DECENCY

It is very important for a maid to be decent or neat in appearance. In whatever environment you find yourself as a maid in service, it could be in the church, in business, in your home, it is important for you to look decent. Your appearance as a maidservant is very important. It is said that beauty is in the eye of the beholder which means to some people you may be beautiful but others may say you are not. But if you are a neat and decent person, it will definitely show and it can not be debated. People will appreciate you and the service rendered. Also, in the execution of your duties as a maid and for the service rendered to be acceptable, a maid should ensure that the materials for disposing such duties are kept clean. For example, as a maid when serving your master a glass of water, it is expected that the glass and water should be clean and served in a presentable form. It is not an issue of putting gold apparels to prove your attractiveness but just be neat. As a church secretary and administrator with a family to cater for, I have come to realise that physical neatness is more important than the cost or quality of the clothes I put on. With my obligation to assist my husband in the financial running of the home, I ensure that my work clothes are maintained to high standard for them to serve longer than to go on a shopping spree every now and then in other to look new. It is unwise to put your family finances in jeopardy all because you want to look expensive at all times in the bid to impress people. But it is required of a maidservant to look neat and to dress decently at all times.

Moreover, as a worker in church working directly with a man of God, it is important to apply caution in choosing your wardrobe. Please, kindly exercise decency when doing this. By popular opinion, men are easily attracted by what they see. Clothes that reveal sensitive parts of the body should not be worn. Such clothes could be exposing some major parts of your chest level and thereby revealing a part of your breasts or trousers that are tight fitting revealing the lines of your underwear. Some trousers are supposed to have belt holes but due to some decisions by the designer, they are not there. How about the g-strings pants? This could easily be seen by the master during the course of service most especially when the maid squats. Some Masters could be very embarrassed at this kind of outlook and the embarrassment could be severe especially when there are guests being entertained in his office. Maids, be very careful when choosing your wardrobe as suggestive outlook can be detrimental to the performance of your God given services and do not let your actions jeopardise the future of your master and his God given vision as God will strongly hold you accountable.

As a maid, one of the ways by which your level of understanding of spiritual holiness is portrayed is in your physical appearance and this can be seen in the scripture:

1 Timothy 2:9, "in like manner also, that the women adorn themselves in modest apparel, with propriety and moderation, not with braided hair or gold or pearls or costly clothing, [10] *but, which is proper for women professing godliness, with good works."*

HUMILITY

Humility is an important quality of a godly maid. Godly humility is being comfortable with who you are in the Lord and putting others first. Godly humility leads to wisdom.

Phil. 2:3-4, "Let nothing be done through selfish ambition or conceit, but in lowliness of mind let each esteem others better than himself. 4 Let each of you look out not only for his own interests, but also for the interests of others.

How can a maid exercise the spirit of humility in carrying out her services? By putting others first and knowing who you are in Christ. Knowing who you are in Christ will enable you not to fight back but pursue peace. It is the spirit of a peacemaker. Not saying a word of defence back to your master in a tensed atmosphere, even when you know you are right but have not been asked to speak is a sign of humility. In this situation, you could go to him or her when the atmosphere is calm and explain the situation to him or her. Jesus Christ demonstrated a good example of humility by washing the disciples' feet. A maid carrying the masters' bag despite the weight is a sign of humility. Though, it is not on her job description but she has to bow low and carry the bag either to the office or to the car. This is a sign of godly humility that earns a desirable reward. It is difficult to accord someone respect on a daily basis without exercising the spirit of humility. Some people say respect is reciprocal but not in all cases. You may have an arrogant master who exercises his arrogance towards you because of your position and seldom treats you with respect but treats others that come his way with much respect. This should not stop you from being respectful. It is better for you to leave him or her to God and if you can not bear it, you are free to change your job. God will reward everyone accordingly.

Galatians 6:7 Do not be deceived, God is not mocked; for whatever a man sows, that he will also reap.

As a maid, for you to succeed well in carrying out your responsibility and make a difference, you must possess the spirit of humility.

Also, as a maid, show respect and be humble in your dealings with other maids especially those you meet in service or are older than you. These are your navigators in your master's house.

They will render every necessary assistance required by you in order for you to familiarise yourself quickly with the new environment. This will bring promotion and elevation your way speedily than you think. Never look down on them because you may never get to the top and even if you do, it will not last. When you start falling, there will be no one beneath to show you mercy and take you in.

A maid that desires to be great must have the desire to serve. Never feel too big to serve or else you may equally be too small to lead. If you desire to lead others, you must humble yourself and serve them first.

QUIET

A Maid should not be talkative. In any capacity a maid serves either in her master's house, in the ministry, office or in the farmland, it is important she possesses a quiet spirit.

Proverbs 13:3 "He who guards his mouth preserves his life, but he who opens wide his lips shall have destruction."

By reason of her service, a maid may have access to official information about the ministry or office she serves. A maid that is a talkative will end up releasing vital information that may be detrimental to the master's personality, family, business or ministry. A maid that is a talkative can destroy so many things and it may be too late before she realises it.

Proverbs 10:19 In the multitude of words sin is not lacking, but he who restrains his lips is wise.

A quiet maid will have tendencies to be articulate, constructive and coordinate. Quietness also helps to conserve energy to carry out your duties. Talkativeness drains the energy available for the daily task. When a maid spends her energy talking, she ends up losing the strength to carry out her duties. She falls easily into a state of exhaustion and the stamina required for the main job is gone. This slows down and reduces productivity and in no time, the maid can be ordered out of her job.

Also, it is important that a maid that desires to see and enjoy good days in her Master's house should keep a close watch over her lips in other to prevent it from speaking evil or deceit. This equally applies to everyone and it is an instruction from the holy bible.

Psalm 34:12 -13 "Who is the man who desires life, and loves many days, that he may see good?
13 Keep your tongue from evil, and your lips from speaking deceit.

1Peter 3:10 "For He who would love life And see good days, Let him refrain his tongue from evil, and his lips from speaking deceit.

GENTLENESS

A maid should be gentle. Gentleness is a fruit of the Holy Spirit. It is of importance to a maid that wants to enjoy the position God has placed her to desire the manifestation of such fruit. It will be seen in her actions, words and conversation. *AN UNGENTLE MAID SPILLS HER MILK OVER.*

As a maid, be gentle in your actions especially when you have been offended by someone. It is important you do not react immediately but politely respond. I learned from my master that in such a situation, I should count ten fingers before uttering a word. This means before you finish counting your ten fingers, your emotions would have been brought under control and you are likely not to regret your response. He made me understand that when you react immediately, you may utter words that cannot be withdrawn because words are like eggs. Shells of broken eggs cannot be amended and brought back to the original state so are spoken words. Immediately when spoken, it will be difficult to erase them from the hearts of the recipients. Whether you are hurt deliberately or not, avoid reacting in a negative manner that will put your Christian belief or maturity in doubt.

HOSPITALITY:

A good maid regardless of her age should be hospitable. Her hospitality should not only be towards her master but towards everyone within the master's house and visitors to the master's house and by so doing, she is able to win the hearts of people within and outside and thereby help to create a wall of defence for herself on the day of evil and also receive a blessing from an unexpected source. In the scriptures, we find a similar example in the life of Sarah and Abraham who entertained Angels and God visited them that same year.

Genesis 18:6-10, "So Abraham hurried into the tent to Sarah and said, "Quickly, make ready three measures of fine meal; knead it and make cakes." [7] And Abraham ran to the herd, took a tender and good calf, gave it to a young man, and he hastened to prepare it. [8] So he took butter and milk and the calf which he had prepared, and set it before them; and he stood by them under the tree as they ate. [9] Then they said to him, "Where is Sarah your wife?" So he said, "Here, in the tent." [10] And He said, "I will certainly return to you according to the time of life, and behold, Sarah your wife shall have a son."

Being a good hospitable character, Rebecca found a husband. If you are single, it is important you develop high level of hospitality. You will enjoy more favour and attraction from the opposite sex and you will not wait for too long to see the wedding bells ring. God will single you out for the best in the name of Jesus, Amen. Another example is the widow of Zarephath during the time of Elisha. There were so many widows during that time but God sent Elisha to her because He is the one that knows and sees the hearts of all men. The woman did not relent but rather gave up her meal for the prophet and God Almighty surprised her. What can we say about the couple that entertained the Prophet yearly in their house and yet without a child, Jehovah Jireh (the Provider), surprised them by honouring the word of His servant.

Hospitality is a very good quality. Also a woman that possesses this gift will be able to defend her family on the day of wrath. This can be seen in the story of David, Nabal and Abigail in the book of

1Samuel 25: 1-32, "Then Abigail made haste and took two hundred loaves of bread, two skins of wine, five sheep already

dressed, *five seahs of roasted grain, one hundred clusters of raisins, and two hundred cakes of figs, and loaded them on donkeys.* ¹⁹ *And she said to her servants, "Go on before me; see, I am coming after you." But she did not tell her husband Nabal."*

*"*³² *Then David said to Abigail: "Blessed is the LORD God of Israel, who sent you this day to meet me!* ³³ *And blessed is your advice and blessed are you, because you have kept me this day from coming to bloodshed and from avenging myself with my own hand.* ³⁴ *For indeed, as the LORD God of Israel lives, who has kept me back from hurting you, unless you had hurried and come to meet me, surely by morning light no males would have been left to Nabal!"*

Abigail's hospitality was a defence for Nabal when David wanted to strike.

As a maid, be very hospitable. First impression matters a lot and you may not have the opportunity to do it the second time most especially to the visitors and what will they say about you? What recommendations are you expecting that will take you to the top? You are not far from them if you are hospitable.

ENERGETIC

Just as the word goes, a maid must be energetic. You must be full of energy: physical, spiritual and financial energy. As a maid for the past eight years, I have realised that in other for me to serve very well, I must maintain my energy level. Due to high level of demand placed on me, it is necessary I keep watch over this area. It is important as a maid to eat well most especially before you set out to do any task because this will keep you going until you are able to "refuel". The people you are serving may not know what is going on with you and their concern at that moment is for you to meet their demand at that particular time. Without anything in the belly, you will only manage for a while and before you know it, you will begin to carry a gloomy face and this causes faster release of adrenalin and thereby resulting to inexplicable anger. David wanted to kill Nabal because he was hungry and his demand for some food and meat was not met and he had been toiling all day.

It is also important as a maid to be involved in regular exercises to keep your heart alive. A good walkout can help you to decongest the burden you carry. As an Administrator, this helps me a great deal. Every weight that may have been transferred to me from my master, colleagues and members of the church are easily gotten off my mind when I go for a walkout.

Spiritual energy is also needed to enable success as a maid. This energy does not run dry. No man can comprehend it. People just wonder at the level of its operation in your life. Anyone God has chosen for this great work will be given this type of energy. If you are a worker in His house, you need this type of energy. It flows when others are tired. It is the energy required to go extra mile, it is the energy required to face the devil. While Jesus Christ waited before His betrayal, the disciples slept but He said:

Luke 22:46: "Then He said to them, "Why do you sleep? Rise and pray, lest you enter into temptation."

You need to seek consistently spiritual powers and authorities from God to enable you surmount problems or issues that may arise daily. The scripture says in:

2 Corinthians 10:4-6, "For the weapons of our warfare are not carnal but mighty in God for pulling down strongholds, [5] casting down arguments and every high thing that exalts itself against the knowledge of God, bringing every thought into captivity to the obedience of Christ, [6] and being ready to punish all disobedience when your obedience is fulfilled."

Looking at the office structure, the maid receives more callers than the master. The master will only see those on his appointment list for that day, those he will like to see or a genuine emergency. For the maid to deal with everyone in an agreeable and acceptable manner, she needs spiritual energy. For one to say "no" to a stubborn spirit and it responds immediately requires a backup from God. The church today is so imperfect to the extent that possessors of contrary spirits find it comfortable to dwell in it and as an Administrator, I have found out so well that one needs more of spiritual energy than ever.

There are people that just want to come in and drain you but God will always proved Himself strong. In any capacity you are serving, you need spiritual energy. If you lack this in your life, do not hesitate to ask for it. He will supply you.

Matthew 7:7: "Ask, and it will be given to you; seek, and you will find; knock, and it will be opened to you."

James 1:5: "If any of you lacks wisdom, let him ask of God, who gives to all liberally and without reproach, and it will be given to him.

A maid needs financial energy. Gone are those days when a maid spends her finances on herself and family alone. The relationship that last longer today is a symbiotic one. God has moved us from the lowest level to a level of recognition and our identity in Christ has made the difference. No matter your earnings, you should be able to use your finance to assist in the execution of your master's goals and vision. A financial issue may arise in the organisation and your master is not available to resolve the issue, but you may have the resource to solve it, please do not hesitate to do so. All we have comes from God and such actions will only add value to you rather than diminish you. By doing so, your master will feel in his heart that your relationship with him is not just for your gain only but a much and deeper interest to see his vision come into reality.

Also, be a source of financial blessing to your master or mistress. Give to him or her financially within your capacity and appreciate him or her whenever the need arises. This is a seed that will soon yield a harvest. It is important you appreciate him and his family anytime God lays it in your heart to do so. Don't let their birthdays go unnoticed. Kindly send at least a card. If you are working as a full time staff, it is important you understand that you are serving someone that operates on a dual capacity in your life and this makes his or her position very paramount. He is your Pastor and your boss and by reason of growth in the relationship, he becomes a very close friend and can relate on a very close capacity. You spend more time with him in the office than anyone else. Be very careful how you treat him. Be generous towards him and beloved, remember, the more you give, the more you receive and God will enrich you more by providing for you and you will have plenty left over to share with others.

As a maid, let this be your prayer point that God will make you a source of financial blessing to your master and his ministry. Moreover, it should be the prayer of every maid especially those serving in the house of God, that God should increase their sources of income. Even as a wife, you don't have to wait for your husband to give you money before you will be able to provide the least thing at home. Exercise the qualities of the woman that was spoken about in Proverbs 31 and God will uphold you.

INITIATIVE

A maid must possess a high level of initiative. As a growing child, my dad's daily sermon was always on initiative and its rewards. My dad dislikes someone that lacked initiative or possesses a low level of it. From childhood, I knew very well that to be a distinct person, you must possess high level of initiative. In the world we are in today, we need to make a difference. As a maid, don't wait to be told to do assignments that are right under "your nose" or probably your eyes have seen them and you know very well, they need to be done. Don't wait for your master to ask you to do it before you respond. In the Ministry, Maids are expected to do so many things and even those outside their job specifications but bear in mind that as you do these so also God will release rewards outside your terms of contract to you in the name of Jesus, Amen. I am a living example of His blessing and I am not afraid to tell you that God will definitely reward. Though, it could be difficult, do not relent, just keep doing what is right and give your best to the service.

LOYALTY

A maid should be loyal to her master. Loyalty is faithfulness or devotion to a person or a group of persons. A loyal maid is faithful and devoted to the master. It shows how willing a maid is by making personal sacrifices in other to build and strengthen the relationship between her and her master.

A maid should be ready to defend her master at any time with everything she possesses. Don't criticise him especially when you are not in support of his ideas. The only responsibility you have in that regard is to pray for him that God directs him to make the best decision because even if he fails, you still owe him your support. You are with him in the boat and it is important that you all get the boat to anchor safely. To avoid capsizing, confusion or creating an atmosphere for the devil to send a terrible storm against the ministry, you must support him more in prayers and render scriptural advice on the condition that your opinion or advice is requested for.

True loyalty is a rare quality among many servants today and this is as a result of lack of clarity in a master's visions and goals, a break down in the lines of communication, distractions, insecurity, a master's lack of integrity and credibility and many more.

As a Christian, there is no excuse for divided loyalty in service. Whenever you encounter such issues as a maid let Christ occupy the middle. Let Him be your centre focus in other to cover those elements that may cause you to become disloyal. When you see Jesus Christ in the situation, you will not be able see your master's weaknesses and before you know it, the issues will be resolved without creating a rancour.

For example, a maid begins to feel insecure in the hands of a master that makes promises to reward her good works but fails to do so. A feeling of insecurity is created in the life of maid by a master that lacks integrity and credibility. When a master gives excuses for his inability to fulfil a promise but does not find it difficult meeting his own needs and satisfaction he is merely displaying his level of reliability and dependability.

Maid, never rely or depend on anyone for your reward. It is calamitous to put your hope in man. Put your hope in God. Place your expectations on Him. As His child, it is important that your security should be in Him. He is the only one that rewards true loyalty and He will surely reward you if you don't wobble. Jonathan was a true and loyal friend of David and gave up the throne for him. He never saw David as a threat to his future destiny as king of Israel but was loyal to the end. Though, he was not alive to enjoy the reward but the day the book of remembrance was opened, David remembered the house of Saul (Jonathan's father) in other to reward Jonathan for all he sacrificed for him. Though, people in this class of Jonathan's loyalty are very few today but this is the best example of genuine loyalty which we are to emulate.

2 Samuel 9:1-7, "Now David said, "Is there still anyone who is left of the house of Saul, that I may show him kindness for Jonathan's sake?" 2 And there was a servant of the house of Saul whose name was Ziba. So when they had called him to David, the king said to him, "Are you Ziba?" He said, "At your service!" 3 Then the king said, "Is there not still someone of the house of Saul, to whom I may show the kindness of God?" And Ziba said to the king," There is still a son of Jonathan who is lame in his feet." 4 So the king said to him, "Where is he?" And Ziba said to the king, "Indeed he is in the house of Machir the son of Ammiel, in Lo Debar." 5 Then King David sent and brought him out of the house of Machir the son of Ammiel, from Lo Debar. 6 Now when Mephibosheth the son of Jonathan, the son of Saul, had come to David, he fell on his face and prostrated himself. Then David said, "Mephibosheth?" And he answered, "Here is your servant!" [7] So David said to him, "Do not fear, for I will surely show you kindness for Jonathan your father's sake, and will restore to you all the land of Saul your grandfather; and you shall eat bread at my table continually."

Though Jonathan died but God preserved Mephiboseth's life in other for him to harvest the fruits of his father's loyalty to David. Beloved, you will not only enjoy the benefits for being loyal but your generation will also enjoy it.

Another good example of loyalty based on servanthood is the loyalty of Abraham's servant towards Abraham. He sworn to Abraham that he would ensure that Isaac does not marry among the Canaanites and he ensured he got wife for Isaac from his kindred even when Abraham was dead. This servant was loyal to Abraham even in death.

Genesis 24: "1 Now Abraham was old, well advanced in age; and the Lord had blessed Abraham in all things. 2 So Abraham said to the oldest servant of his house, who ruled over all that he had, "Please, put your hand under my thigh, 3 and I will make you swear by the Lord, the God of heaven and the God of the earth, that you will not take a wife for my son from the daughters of the Canaanites, among whom I dwell; 4 but you shall go to my country and to my family, and take a wife for my son Isaac."

10 Then the servant took ten of his master's camels and departed, for all his master's goods were in his hand. And he arose and went to Mesopotamia, to the city of Nahor. 11 And he made his camels kneel down outside the city by a well of water at evening time, the time when women go out to draw water. 12 Then he said, "O Lord God of my master Abraham, please give me success this day, and show kindness to my master Abraham. 13 Behold, here I stand by the well of water, and the daughters of the men of the city are coming out to draw water. 14 Now let it be that the young woman to whom I say, 'Please let down your pitcher that I may drink,' and she says, 'Drink, and I will also give your camels a drink' — let her be the one You have appointed for Your servant Isaac. And by this I will know that You have shown kindness to my master."

15 And it happened, before he had finished speaking, that behold, Rebekah, who was born to Bethuel, son of Milcah, the wife of Nahor, Abraham's brother, came out with her pitcher on her shoulder.

66 And the servant told Isaac all the things that he had done. 67 Then Isaac brought her into his mother Sarah's tent; and he took Rebekah and she became his wife, and he loved her. So Isaac was comforted after his mother's death.

TRUSTWORTHY

It is one of the spices of any good and interesting relationship and it is very delicate. Good relationships are built on trust. It means belief, faith, certainty, assurance, convictions, and reliance. To be employed to serve a master requires trust and to be the bridegroom's choice of a bride also requires trust. No man will like to marry a woman that was deceitful during courtship. As a staff in an office, you occupy a position of trust. It is a dangerous thing to betray trust. Trust betrayed can destroy destiny. It can turn your destiny helper against you. My Pastor always say to me that when trust is betrayed, it will require time and other resources to rebuild it. It takes a great deal of time to build trust when it's betrayed. As a maid, be trustworthy. Ensure that the trust placed on you by your master gets to a level that he can confidently defend you when faced with false accusations. Every maid serving a Man of God should be very careful. Men of God can easily forgive but God will always fight for them. When you are occupying a position of trust, guide it with the fear of God in your mind. Execute your job by bearing in mind always that God is watching. Never do anything contrary or detrimental either by reason of life pressures or greed. If you urgently need financial help, it is better you ask than to steal. If you are shy or afraid to ask, then you can pray intensively about it and you will be surprised that God will intervene as long as your intention is right. I am a living testimony of this. Most blessings I have enjoyed as a maid have always been by praying to God. I have always found it hard to ask but my Pastor will always insist I ask especially when it is a burden in my heart. Maid of God, remember always that man can always render help within their limits but God's help knows no limit and there is no pay back. Please never you steal from your master and do not betray your master as Judas Iscariot did to our Lord Jesus Christ. A maid that steals from her master or betrays her master by releasing information that can destroy him has robbed herself of a generational blessing. Please learn to maintain confidentiality.

COURTEOUS

It is important for a maid to be courteous. It means a maid has to be polite, well-mannered, civil, respectful, well-behaved, well-bred, and gracious, considerate, pleasant, polished, refined and civilized. In any capacity you are serving as a maid, you should be courteous.

In an office where you have more than one maid, the master will often prefer the most courteous maid to attend to high ranking visitors to his office. That's his choice and it's a good one. Maid, endeavour to look good always in your appearance, service delivery and in speech and you will enjoy its benefits. Keep abreast of information that will enhance your development in order to serve better and serve in any capacity.

MINISTRY OF A MAID

The maid has a broad ministry. The master does not allow everyone working under him to serve him directly even if they are working in his house. There are maids that serve at the gate, there are maids that serve in the courtyards and there are maids that serve in the inner chambers. I termed the various levels of service as the ministry of the maid. Irrespective of the level at which you have been called to serve, you have been placed there by God and you will be accountable to your master and your eternal master Jesus Christ. Be faithful to your calling.

Maids that work in the gates are the first receivers of visitors to the master's house and it is their duty to ensure that the compound is clean and beautiful at all times. Their job is to ensure that callers to their master's territory have a good impression about the environment. A first impression on the hearts of callers about your master's house is very important. There may never be a second chance to make corrections. Bear in mind always that first impression is a lasting impression. It is important you make the environment a welcoming and a friendly one. The outlook of the area may vary but regardless of how much your master could afford to spend to ensure its beauty, the type of spirit in the environment will determine how people will feel when they come in. Therefore, as a maid working in this area, it is important you saturate the atmosphere, the room and yourself daily with the power of the Holy Spirit. Learn to pray daily in your work environment and invite the presence of the Holy Spirit to fill the room and take charge of the day. Do you know that the outlook and presence of the power of God in this area of your master's territory can bring about elevation to your master's business? People that could be of help to the vision of your master can walk into this area and by reason of the way they have been received; they will not leave until they have rendered that help. But if it's the contrary, the vision of your master will suffer some delays and setbacks which may also affect you.

This area is very important. Workers in this section should be very careful and must have a good attitude. Be cheerful. If you are the type that wears makeup, wear it moderately. It is important you look good, smart and courteous. Occasionally, people may come to you seeking help that may not be your responsibility to render, especially financial assistance. If you have the means, do not pass the responsibility to somebody else. It is a seed; it will definitely germinate and bring forth harvest.

Maids that work in the courtyard are those that work within the building but may not work directly with the master. They are serving the master by working on how the master's goals and visions can be actualised. They create or set strategies on how the master's visions and goals can be executed. These maids need a high level of concentration, must be energetic and truthful. It is important that maids under this category state genuinely the facts of information within their reach and present such facts to their master without altering them. But it is very unfortunate today; some maids in this section sometimes align information received with their own vision or goals and present it to the master as facts gathered to execute a strategy. This is as a result of selfish ambition. As a maid, never serve in order to actualise your selfish ambition. When you do so, you would have offended three categories of people: God, your earthly master and his subjects. They will not be pleased with you. If you are in the office where policies, strategies, planning are written, please be very careful else the boat will be navigated to a wrong destination.

Maids that work in the inner chambers work directly with the master. In any organisation especially the church, they are very few. Such people serve the master directly and they have access to him. Their jobs are very sensitive and they are required to possess a higher level of trust than the maids in the other two categories. They serve the master's meal; drinks, tidy up his office, open his personal mails, and know a lot of things about his private life. Sometimes, the maid may know something about the master that no other person may know. Never discuss this with anyone. Such information must go to the grave with you. This category of maids also knows the master's strengths and weaknesses but it is very dangerous and satanic to expose such weakness before another person. It is important you report a destructive weakness to a higher authority or his wife. Let your approach to such issue be very constructive and not destructive.

It is of great importance for any maid in this level to be very protective of the master. You must be his shield always. Maids in the inner chambers also have the responsibility of ensuring that the master's appearance is right for every occasion. Ensure he is well dressed, perfumed and nice looking. Don't let the man of God go out shabbily without letting him know that he needs some fixing. There is no sin in it. You are doing your job but be very careful of your motive and if he feels uncomfortable at such gestures, find an alternative way of passing the information to him; possibly through a male employee or servant in the vineyard. Sometimes, some people lack understanding of such issue and tend to view it as an occasion to become jealous but maid, regardless of anyone's opinion about your protective nature of your master, don't let him fall into the dragnet of the devil. Always remember that you have a bigger master in heaven that you are accountable to.

2 Corinthians 2:11, "lest Satan should take advantage of us; for we are not ignorant of his devices."

John 10:10, "The thief does not come except to steal, and to kill, and to destroy. I have come that they may have life, and that they may have it more abundantly."

Being a maid that has served her master for a couple of years, I understood from the onset that God has committed a great destiny into my hands and it is my responsibility to protect such a destiny. I know on the last day, He will surely ask me how I was able to handle such a great destiny.

Moreover, be your master's defender and not his destroyer. Please do not become a dark cloud over his destiny or a blackmailer. Your assignment to work with him is arranged by God. It is a proof that God trusts you and has destined you at a particular stage in your life to handle such a great responsibility. When you betray him, you betray God. If your master is married and has children, bear in mind the day you betray him, you will be shocked that you have hurt not just one person but a group. You become an enemy of his wife, children and the entire church. The guilt you will feel is more severe than the damage you have done and it will take the grace of God for you to forgive yourself. You may not know it but to be forewarned is to be forearmed. Rather than you betraying your master, it is better for you to quit the job.

Maids, please never take side with anyone against your master especially when issues are brought before you that may indicate some lapses or negligence on your master's part. Be his defence especially in his absence and ensure loopholes are covered. Whatever you cannot do or say in his presence, never do or say in his absence.

Five

MAID! OCCUPY YOUR PLACE

As a maid, it is important you occupy your place. The word "occupy" can be defined in different ways but in this contest, it means to hold or fill a position or an office. In order to occupy your place as a maid, it will require you to acquire some certain degree of knowledge necessary for the execution of your job, wisdom and insight to handle daily issues and a discerning spirit to be able to instantly differentiate the good from evil.

HOW CAN A MAID OCCUPY HER PLACE?

In ministry, a maid can occupy her place by:

1. **Being knowledgeable in the word of God:** It is very important as a maid to have a good knowledge and understanding of the word of God and be able to analyse and apply the word of God accurately.

2 Timothy 4:1-5, "I charge you therefore before God and the Lord Jesus Christ, who will judge the living and the dead at His appearing and His kingdom: ² Preach the word! Be ready in season and out of season. Convince, rebuke, exhort, with all longsuffering and teaching. ³ For the time will come when they will not endure sound doctrine, but according to their own desires, because they have itching ears, they will heap up for themselves teachers; ⁴ and they will turn their ears away from the truth, and be turned aside to fables. ⁵ But you be watchful in all things, endure afflictions, do the work of an evangelist, fulfil your ministry.

In the house of God, people will come to you with different issues but the difference between you and the maid in the secular world will be your approach to such issue. Your ability to apply the word of God in bringing solution to such issues makes the difference. If you review issues with the eye of the world, you have failed in occupying your place spiritually. As a maid of God, you are an Evangelist and an Ambassador. You must possess a good knowledge of the Word of God. It is important you study the bible regularly and let your counsel be directed by the Word of God. 2 Timothy 2:15

2. **Acquiring a suitable formal education:** As a maid, in other for you to occupy your place, endeavour to develop yourself by acquiring formal education. Ensure you possess a certain level of education required to meet the needs of majority of your master's subjects. This is not a prerequisite but an advice. If you are serving under a master whose followers are mainly school certificate holders, your minimum qualification should be a first degree. If the majority are first degree holders, you should have a master's degree. If you are on the same level with them, you may not have the capability to deliver something new to them or your capability may not be sufficient. Followers will want to associate

more with a maid that is well informed because they believe she may possess something that they need. This should not result into a show off or arrogance but it is important you have a good academic profile and it is best when your profile carries with it the fruits and power of the Holy Spirit.

3. **Be Informed:** Being well informed of the daily activities and issues in your internal and external environment. In order for you to occupy your place, it is important you have up to date information about your environment both internal and external. Develop the habit of wanting to know the wellbeing of your master or his followers without infringing into their privacy. Have up to date information about activities or events going on in the organisation through appropriate channels and not through gossiping. In your external environment, try as much as possible to gather information that will be a blessing to your master and his followers. Circulate information that you know is vital to the

wellbeing of your master's followers. Don't keep such vital information to yourself.

James 4:17, "Therefore, to him who knows to do good and does not do it, to him it is sin."

Luke 12:47, "And that servant who knew his master's will, and did not prepare himself or do according to his will, shall be beaten with many stripes."

Maids, learn to do good. If you have applied information that worked out well for you, do not conceal it, teach others.

4. **Being sensitive:** Maid, in order to occupy your place, be at alert always and let your ears, eyes, nose be very active. Learn to hear deeper than others, see farther than others and smell very quickly than others. Be very sensitive. Learn to develop spiritual antenna. When you possess this, people will begin to imagine how you knew certain things faster than them. There is hardly an event that passes by in my place of service that I am not aware of. I would have received a

revelation of what the outcome will look like. I either dream of it or be uncomfortable about certain aspect. Until it is fixed I am not comfortable and when overlooked, most likely causes mishap. Maid, you have to be very sensitive.

5. **Developing your core gift:** To occupy your place as a maid, develop your core gift. The development of your gift will bring you promotion, recognition and reward. As you render your service to your master, there may be a gift God may have deposited in your life for the edification of the body of Christ and for your blessing.

1 Corinthians 12: 4-7, "There are diversities of gifts, but the same Spirit. 5 There are differences of ministries, but the same Lord. 6 And there are diversities of activities, but it is the same God who works all in all. 7 But the manifestation of the Spirit is given to each one for the profit of all."

It is of great necessity for a maid to desire and develop spiritual gifts in other to occupy her place.

1Corithians 14:1: "Pursue love, and desire spiritual gifts, but especially that you may prophesy".

By developing and using that gift for the benefit of the body of Christ, you are equally adding value to the pursuit of your master's vision and encouraging other helpers of destiny that God may have sent his way. Never put your interest forward when using your gift because it was given you by God first for the profit of all and then you. Remember, it is not yours but God's and it is for the profit of all. "All" means the body of Christ.

Proverbs 18:16, "A man's gift makes room for him, And brings him before great men."

Joseph first of all used his God given gift to interpret dream in the prison before he got a recommendation to the palace and his gift made room for him in the palace.

Genesis 40:8, "We both had dreams," they answered, "but there is no one to interpret them." Then Joseph said to them, "Do not interpretations belong to God? Tell me your dreams."

Genesis 41:14-16 "Then Pharaoh sent and called Joseph, and they brought him quickly out of the dungeon; and he shaved, changed his clothing, and came to Pharaoh. ¹⁵ And Pharaoh said to Joseph, "I have had a dream, and there is no one who can interpret it. But I have heard it said of you that you can understand a dream, to interpret it." ¹⁶ So Joseph answered Pharaoh, saying, "It is not in me; God will give Pharaoh an answer of peace."

6. **Remembering always that you were chosen by God:** In occupying your place as a maid, remember God has appointed and anointed you for that position. God's oil upon your life will strengthen you to do more than your expectations. When you understand your appointment and anointing, you will not be pushed about by people. I have seen in Ministry today that some followers dictate to the maid rather than suggesting ways certain things should be done. This category of people has certain traits that are ungodly. Their goals are to prove that it is their business, they have right to instruct you, place a

demand on you and treat you and the office you occupy without respect. As a maid, do not give in to such personal gains oppressions. Some of this people are demonic agents sent by the devil to frustrate your efforts. Do not yield to their intimidation but rather deal with such people by renewing your boldness in the Lord through prayer and politely rebuking them.

7. **Placing high value on yourself:** In other for you to occupy your place, you need to value yourself. It is the level of value that you place on yourself that people will follow. This value can also be described as self-esteem. If you don't value yourself, no one will value you. Due to some people's negative perception of the nature of the job of a maid, they tend to look down on people occupying such position. It is as a result of this that you must ensure you do not lose your self-esteem in other for people to treat you with respect. You may be a maid but you are a child of the greatest King that has ever reigned and still reigning. You are the princess of God. Occupy

your place as a princess and His glory upon your life will continue to manifest. Do not allow people to relegate you. Whoever relegates you relegates your earthly master that employed you and your heavenly master that placed you there by reason of destiny. Be wise. Kindly digest this wisdom pill: *if you don't want to lose your gate, let no one relegate you.* They will try incessantly but never give up. Maintain your position with great dignity and persistence and in no long a time, they will bow. Do not give up. I pray that where you have been relegated, there you will also be lifted.

Six

THE HURTS

The hurts in the heart of a maid is a chapter of this book that would have been a book on its own, but this book will not be complete without mentioning this aspect in servant hood.

Hurt means to cause bodily injury or pain. It can also mean to damage or decrease the efficiency of a material object by rough use or improper care. In this context, the latter will suffice. As a godly master, do you know your maid could be hurting?

How can a maid be hurt? A maid can be hurt through unfair treatment, injustice, serving a master that lacks integrity thereby leading to unfulfilled promises, abuse etc.

- **UNFAIR TREATMENT**

A master may treat his maid unfairly by undermining, humiliating and intimidating his maid. It also means to treat a maid less favourably than others.

Unfair treatment is very common. Masters should watch out so as not to treat their maids unfairly. Do unto others what you want them to do to you. A master should never take the grace of service rendered by his maid for granted. It is an error when a master perceives the total obedience of a maid as stupidity. When a master compels a maid to do every task without considering her level of strength and ignore the fact that she needs to rest, the maid will be hurt. It is worse when she finds it difficult to say "No". She thinks that when she says "no" this will make her master feel that she's disobedient. Beloved, this is a wrong notion or a wrong mind-set that will end up destroying your ability to say "no" in situation where it is meant to be said. Moreover, your power of choice will be affected and lastly, whenever you are in your master's presence, he will begin to create task or job where there is none. He will begin to think of an assignment to give to you because he knows you will not say "no" to him. Servant hood does not mean you should lose your ability to say "no" but say it with respect.

Some of the reasons for unfair treatment are tribal (different ethnic or racial background), level in spiritual cadre (a worker in the church and not an ordained minister), financial capacity (do not have other sources of income) and level of giving (not able to give much of financial assistance to the master's vision compare to others).

- **LACK OF INTEGRITY AND UNFULFILLED PROMISES**

Integrity is a good moral value that should be possessed by every child of God but most importantly by people occupying a position of leadership. It means to be honest, upright and having high level adherence to moral principles or ethics that can't be broken in any difficult situation.

Masters should possess integrity especially in the church. Keep your word. Let your "yes" be "yes" and "no" be "no". Masters that make promises to their maids in other to win their hearts and eventually fail to fulfil such promise lack integrity. Such actions will cause a maid to be hurt and this may also cause a master to suffer a bigger loss in the future. I have observed that "God sent" maids are very few but the masters that have them should not take them for granted. As a master, try your best to fulfil every promise you have made to your maid. Whatever you have promised to give to her, give it regardless of the cost. If the weight of the fulfilment of such promise is too heavy at that particular time, review it very well with your maid and let her take the decision. Do not decide or involve others that were not there from the onset to decide. This is very risky. A master that finds it difficult most times to fulfil a promise should never make one. Sometimes, such promises are made based on feelings or emotion and become difficult when they need to be fulfilled.

Maids look up to their masters with high level of belief in them (as men of God that cannot lie). When promises are unfulfilled, then hope is deferred and hope deferred makes the heart sick and a sick heart will become bitter when it cannot forgive. A bitter heart will begin to think of negative actions. This is a very bad state. We must all avoid it as Christians.

- **SEXUAL ABUSE**

Sexual abuse is to involve someone into sexual activity against their will. Due to the pressure applied, the victim does not have the capability to control the situation or the circumstance where the sexual action takes place. In the master and maid relationship, it could be unwanted kissing or touching, unpermitted and violent sexual actions, etc.

Masters that abuse their maids sexually should desist from it. Stop taking undue advantage of your maid else, you will be inviting the wrath of God. Your maid is hurting. Your maid should not become an object of sexual abuse. A man of God that touches his maid in an ungodly manner due to sexual weakness should repent before being exposed. You cannot stand the shame of an uncontrolled or erratic sexual emotions expressed towards a woman that is not your wife.

There are indeed God fearing Masters who understand that such an act is a sin, a sacrilege and also could be demeaning. They guide themselves very well by ensuring they do not fall into such situation. Sexual abuse may not have been experienced by some maids but based on what we hear, we can not be ignorant of the fact that it does not exist in the body of Christ. There may equally be other maids suffering such molestations in silence due to fear and concern for their master. If you are a maid in this category, it is important you flee before it is too late. Don't allow your master to convince you with scriptures. He may know the word of God better than you but lacks the understanding and power there in. Never succumb to such pressures. God may have placed you there to prevent others from pulling him down. Therefore, do not allow the devil to turn you into a vessel for his downfall. If your master refuses to repent or adhere to warnings, run far from him. Discuss with his wife about his weakness but do not go about discussing the act with other people. You don't have the right to destroy a man of God or take vengeance against him. Such issues can be handled in a proper or constructive way. An unrepentant master that is wallowing in sexual sin will be exposed sooner than he thought or his ministry will begin to suffer inexplicable setbacks.

The invisible eye of the Lord is watching you. Stop abusing your maid to avoid being visited by the fire that destroyed Sodom and Gomorrah.

Genesis 19:24,"Then the LORD rained brimstone and fire on Sodom and Gomorrah, from the LORD out of the heavens."

Do you know that when you think or feel you are "using" someone or playing smart and think that the person is not wise and as such, you always have your way, such a one is the worst fool? Avoid being manipulative. It is a very dangerous route.   God is watching.

WHAT CAN HEAL THE HURT?

Healing is a very important process when one is hurt and it is important one goes through it in other to recover. Both parties concerned have roles to play to ensure that the hurt is healed.

THE ROLE OF THE MAID

Maid, if you have been hurt or probably you are still hurting, you will do yourself a lot of good and favour by letting go. It is important you forgive hence you may become bitter. Bitterness will not make you better. It is very dangerous and may lead to emotional and physical harms. Endeavour to get rid of all forms of bitterness that may have developed in your heart.

Ephesians 4:31-32 says "31 Let all bitterness, wrath, anger, clamor, and evil speaking be put away from you, with all malice. 32 And be kind to one another, tender hearted, forgiving one another, even as God in Christ forgave you.

The ways you could eliminate bitterness from your heart are:

1. During conversation with friends or relations, try not to speak words of bitterness.

2. Endeavour not to talk about your past hurts or disappointments. Erase the record of such events from your heart. If you do not do so, you will always be hurt whenever you look back. But if you feel you need to communicate a lesson you may have learned to your audience, then you could talk about it but be careful not to use it to pull anyone down or not to remind yourself of some unpalatable issues.

Isaiah 43:18 says "Do not remember the former things, nor consider the things of old.

3. Having a positive attitude will help to eradicate any negative self-talk or negative thoughts. I have discovered that when one is hurt, this could lead to depression and low self-esteem especially when one's thoughts are geared towards a negative direction. One begins to feel that one was not wise enough. Such feelings will hinder you from seeing a brighter future for yourself. It will diminish your self-esteem and within a short time, you will become a person of low self-esteem. This is very dangerous. The way out of this is for you to maintain a positive attitude by being mindful of your words. Believe that God will do a new thing. Believe in your heart that He will compensate you. Whatever loss you may have incurred or suffered by reason of the hurt, God will compensate you. He is capable of lifting you up where you may have fallen.

    Isaiah 43:19 says "Behold, I will do a new thing, now it shall spring forth; shall you not know it? I will even make a road in the wilderness and rivers in the desert.

A sign of Christian maturity is the ability to remain silent amidst frustrations and not loose one's confidence.

THE ROLE OF THE MASTER

Masters should make efforts to ensure that their maids are happy, are treated with dignity, respect and are not deprived of due benefits. Anything contrary to this is ungodly. A satisfied worker is a dedicated worker. Due to this saying that "oh, it is the work of God", you deprive your maid the benefit accruable or place lesser value on her than others. This has created fear in the hearts of many not to work fulltime in the house of God. In some areas, it has made the job unenviable. Majority prefer to work voluntarily rather than go on fulltime to avoid future disappointment by masters or probably self-guilt if they decide to resign and to sign for secular jobs. They do not want to be trapped and begin to struggle with thoughts of what to do next and how will God feel about it. They prefer not to come in at all than to find themselves mid-way in total jeopardy.

As Christians, it is important that we appreciate those working fulltime in God's vineyard. Express your love and appreciation to such people whenever you have the opportunity to do so. It is a high risk job that touches all aspects of the life of that person. Do not add to their burden but rather be a burden lifter.

Also, a master should know that a maid that watches over his "front" and "back" has been given to him by God. You may be enjoying certain grace or favour by reason of her presence and service in your territory. Endeavour not to treat such maid unjustly. As a master, you will be shocked on the day of calamity; this same maid might be your only helper because God's sent maids know the best and quickest method to open the doors in the master's house more than the master. You may ask "why?" Let's consider the physical doors for example. Have you not observed that most times the doors are already opened before the master arrives and he leaves before they are locked? Even when the door is bad, he may not know except he receives the report. This illustration is applicable to other life settings both positive and negative and she may be your God's sent helper on the day of calamity. Therefore, it is important for a master to treasure his maid.

As a master, don't be a user, be a lifter. A master that lifts his maid can never be forgotten. He will always enjoy mercy and favour. It will be difficult for anyone to understand the secret of his progress in life. He will always operate under open heavens. God will make impossibility to be possible for him because he is not self-centred. These are masters when they move from one level of success to another level; they also move their servant to a new and higher level. This means, the master's success is the maid's success. This is a key in the life of the maid that keeps the hope alive.

2 kings 5:1, "Now Naaman, commander of the army of the king of Syria, was a great and honourable man in the eyes of his master, because by him the LORD had given victory to Syria. He was also a mighty man of valour, but a leper."

He was honourable in the eyes of his master. The bible did not say "in the eyes of a fellow servant". Masters please honour good and faithful servants and this will help strengthen their joy for service. Honouring them should not be when it is only both of you but should also be in public. Publicly honouring a servant is a good morale booster than when done in secret. It makes everyone in your environment both your subjects and visitors to know how much they are valued and thereby raising the level of respect they equally will place on them. This will erase any hurt that may be piling up in their hearts.

Also, masters should make efforts to recognise and reward them often. This should not end with the pay package alone.

In order to enjoy your relationship and increase the longevity of the service of your maids, masters should study their maids and be sensitive to their feelings. Their feelings should not be overlooked. There are concealed issues that cannot be spoken out but cannot be hidden by the entire body. Master, kindly ensure you watch and closely study the face of your maid and be able to tell when she is hurting and do everything within your power to see to it that her joy is restored before she leaves your presence. Just as you are being cared for, it is a good thing to show care towards your maid and by so doing, the tendency of the maid staying longer with you is very high. Be a master that can make a maid to become great in life and not the master that will enslave her forever or enjoy replacement at every short interval. A master that finds it hard to retain a maid for a long period also needs to check his attitude. The master may be a king without the head of a king. He is served by reason of his title or position and not by character. If you are a master but cannot retain a servant, pray that God gives you the true head of a king. You need to know what is expected of you as a master. You are to care for your household including your servants.

Do you also know that there are maids but with the head of a queen? They have good leadership qualities despite their position. They have the power of influence and to turn situations and circumstances round. They can go the extra mile you cannot reach. Sometimes, as a master you cannot go to some places but your maid can go that extra mile for you. It will be difficult for you as a master to meet some certain demands placed on you by your subjects, but your maid can do that on your behalf in other for your subjects to know you care.

In conclusion, my prayer for you as a master is that you will not lose your headship and every expectation placed on you by virtue of your position will be visited by divine ability to enable fulfilment in the name of Jesus Christ. As a maid, if you have been hurt by those you render services to; please forgive them so that you too can enjoy God's forgiveness. If you don't forgive them, you will not be able to enter in to your place of destiny and God's purpose for your life may never be fulfilled. You may change job but this may not change the situation. For the seed of greatness deposited by God in you to manifest, you need to forgive or else you may die a servant.

Matthew 6:15, "But if you do not forgive men their trespasses, neither will your Father forgive your trespasses."

Forgiveness is a command. It is a requirement by God for every believer. If you must enter heaven, do not hold any grudge or bitterness in your heart. Please forgive and move on.

I pray that God Almighty will heal the hearts of maids that are hurting and gives you the grace to forgive those that have hurt you and empowers you to forget your hurts in the name of Jesus Christ, Amen.

Seven

REWARDS

A maid will be rewarded by God and man for the services rendered by her to her master. The reward could either be good or bad.

What is a reward? It has many definitions but in this context, it is defined as what is given for good or evil done or something given or received in recompense for worthy behaviour or in retribution for evil acts. The bible says in *Galatians 6:7-8, "Do not be deceived, God is not mocked; for whatever a man sows, that he will also reap. 8 For he who sows to his flesh will of the flesh reap corruption, but he who sows to the Spirit will of the Spirit reap everlasting life. 9 And let us not grow weary while doing good, for in due season we shall reap if we do not lose heart."*

As a maid if you sow good, you will reap good and if you sow evil, you will also reap evil. Ensure you do everything possible to be good. How can you do good in other for you to reap good? Have a good conscience. Examine your heart and see if you would tolerate the same thing if you were in the position of the master. Listen to your conscience speak to you. This is the voice of the Holy Spirit.

Psalm 19:11, "Moreover by them Your servant is warned, And in keeping them there is great reward."

If you harden your heart and you do evil, your reward will surely come and it may come speedily.

A servant can be rewarded here on earth and in heaven.

2 Samuel 19:36, "Your servant will go a little way across the Jordan with the king. And why should the king repay me with such a reward?"

The king in the scripture above is the master. Sometimes a maid may not enjoy the expected reward here on earth but her generation will, and more so she will enjoy it in heaven. God is the great reward-giver. He will reward everyone according to their deeds.

THE KEYS TO REWARD

1. FAITHFULNESS AND OBEDIENCE

Beloved, God rewards faithfulness and obedience most especially during the period of hardship and heartbreak. In a period of difficulty, the level of faithfulness, commitment and dedication to service of a maid should increase and not diminish. God sees everyone and He will reward accordingly. Based on my years of experience, I have learned that a maid that wants to be appreciated and valued should not become another source of heartache to her master. When your master is experiencing trials in ministry, family or business, do everything within your means to ease his burden. It is the time for you to be faithful and to double your mode of delivery. This will increase your value.

2. UNDERSTAND THAT YOUR MASTER'S CRISIS IS YOUR CRISIS.

Crisis in the ministry especially financial and church break-ups are key issues that may send your master to an untimely death. It is the responsibility of the maid to sit tight and see to it that her master manages these crises with care. Ensure you encourage him with the word of God daily, be strong for him and relieve him from psychological stress by helping to attend to issues that may be his priorities, or else, the church may suffer more and his health may begin to fail and there may not be an opportunity for recovery. By the time God intervenes and turns the situation around, he may not be alive to enjoy the fruits of his labour and you too may not be there. You may be replaced by another maid of the new master. Understand that your master's crisis is your crisis. His joy is your joy. If he enjoys promotion, I believe in my heart that yours is also near. If he receives a gift or gifts, I know that yours is also on the way. Maid support your master always and in life you will also enjoy support both on request and without request and your generation will not lack help.

3. MAKE SACRIFICES

Reward comes by reason of sacrifice or hard work. It is difficult for a master to reward a lazy servant except the reward is a general reward. Even at that, a lazy servant cannot enjoy a general reward for long because no one will like to keep a lazy servant in employment. Sooner or later, she will be sacked and replaced.

Matthew 25:26-30, "But his lord answered and said to him, 'You wicked and lazy servant, you knew that I reap where I have not sown, and gather where I have not scattered seed. 27 So you ought to have deposited my money with the bankers, and at my coming I would have received back my own with interest. 28 Therefore take the talent from him, and give it to him who has ten talents. 29 For to everyone who has, more will be given, and he will have abundance; but from him who does not have, even what he has will be taken away. 30 And cast the unprofitable servant into the outer darkness. There will be weeping and gnashing of teeth."

A maid will enjoy a reward for the time put into her duties. Every unpaid overtime hour worked in the church of God will be put into your account by God. Covenants that you may have made by sacrificing your time to ensure that the work does not suffer will be rewarded.

Some maids decided not to have children in order for the work not to suffer pending when there are available resources to employ and train another maid. This sacrifice will be rewarded. Some decide to space their children to avoid going on maternity leave often for the work not to suffer. Every covenant made by sacrifice will receive a double reward. God is not unjust. You may have made a covenant in the secret, He will reward you openly.

Psalm 50: 5, "Gather My saints together to Me, Those who have made a covenant with Me by sacrifice."

God will reward your labour. Please, don't give up.

HINDERANCES TO REWARD

A maid needs to pray against hindrances to reward. They are both physical and spiritual. There is a group of people that will hear about a planned reward for you and will not be happy. These are people that are skilful in measuring rewards but do not measure the sacrifices that has been made by you. They ignore the sacrifices and begin to ask question such as: why must it be you? Is she the only one there? They don't want to see or hear any reason why you should be given such a reward. Rewards that you may receive or enjoy from an environment like this are rewards that people's opinion was not sought before it was given to you. You need to pray daily against obstacles to your rising, obstacles to your promotion, obstacles to your recognition and obstacles to the manifestations of God's glory in your life and family.

I want to pass this also to people that stand as obstacles to other people's reward. Bear in mind that whatever a man sows, he will reap. It is very dangerous to be an obstacle. Your understanding of the reason why the reward is being made is not necessary at all times. It may be a fulfilment of a promise made to the maid by the master which no other person is aware of or a fulfilment of the person's destiny coming into limelight. God does not request for our permission whenever He wants to bless someone and He can destroy anyone that poses an obstacle. Have you forgotten what happened between Mordecai and Haman in the book of Esther? Anyone that stands as an obstacle to someone else's progress is treading on a dangerous path and it is advisable that such a one should have a change of heart.

I have learnt from my master the in-depth interpretation of this popular scripture in *Galatians 6:7* "......*whatever a man sows, he shall also reap*....." This has helped me to be very careful of the information I pass across to him especially when it relates to the benefits of others."

Please do not be a hindrance or obstacle on the path of the way of someone the king has decided to favour. If you think you deserve such favour and you are not getting it, kindly go on your knees and command the book of remembrance to be opened for you. You will definitely be remembered at the appointed time. You will be surprised at the massive rain of favour that will pour from heaven on you.

REWARD AND ITS TIMING

Rewards may not come at the time expected because God's timetable is different from our timetable. His time is the best. When there are delays in rewards being received, don't give up. It may be delayed but not denied. I know it is hard sometimes when you see that a person that does not sacrifice more time than you is being rewarded or someone that met you in the place of service enjoying more benefits, see it as a test of your patience and perseverance. If you are not patient and you exit by reason of anger or envy, you may miss your reward and it will be given to someone else. My prayer for you is that your reward will not pass you by and that your portion will not be given to someone else in Jesus name, Amen.

In conclusion, for one to enjoy one's service to one's master one should not focus one's mind on material gain.

People that are motivated by material gains or reward can never be satisfied. It is likely they may end like Judas Iscariot. Let God through the help of the Holy Spirit be your key motivator. If your motivation is from God, you will enjoy both material and spiritual satisfaction. You will enjoy what money cannot buy.

As a maid, I have enjoyed rewards from my master and my master's followers. God has placed certain group of people to encourage, lift my hands and head even when I am fainting. Some are there to assist me in my physical needs, some bring me words of encouragement that lift up my spirit and God has used some to bring fulfilment to promises.

Beloved, when you consider God as your master and carry out your duties as if He is your immediate employer, your reward will never pass you by. Where you think you have been deprived, He will bring double reward to you. Maids, strive, make preparations and you will succeed. You will succeed by fulfilling purpose and entering your place of destiny.

Hebrews 6:10-12, "For God is not unjust to forget your work and labour of[a] love which you have shown toward His name, in that you have ministered to the saints, and do minister. 11 And we desire that each one of you show the same diligence to the full assurance of hope until the end, 12 that you do not become sluggish, but imitate those who through faith and patience inherit the promises."

 **Eight**

CONCLUSION

In conclusion, it is very important as a maid to know that your existence is centred on the purpose of God for your life. You are where you are today either because you have discovered God's purpose for your life or you are in the process of discovering it. But it is important that you know the reason why you came to this earth. If you are yet to know, begin to pray about it. Where you are may be a process you need to undergo to enable the fulfilment of your destiny. There are certain things that you need to learn or know in other for you to move to the next level. Until you undergo such process, you will not be able to move to the next level.

- You need to understand that God has deposited a seed of greatness in every human. Don't allow inferiority complex to diminish the potentials God has deposited in you. You need to re-examine yourself and have a clear picture of your self-image. Your service should not destroy your self-esteem. Have self-respect, self –determination, self-ideal and self-discipline. Break free from low self-esteem, mediocrity, financial lack and indiscipline and ensure your desire to improve yourself does not emanate from selfishness.

- Understand that you are the master of your own destiny. Set goals for yourself and be determined to actualise these goals.

- Do not relent in your service. Execute your duties with passion. This passion is a sign of affection towards God. The work you are doing is for the betterment of His kingdom. You cannot say you love God and sees His work as a burden.

- Understand that every task that comes your way is an opportunity for you to express your love towards God. He understands when you are exhausted and cannot take on more tasks and you politely say "no". God is not a man. He knows us more than we do. Never reject tasks arrogantly or by grumbling. This is not proper. The blessings you enjoy today are the products of your labour for God's kingdom on earth. If you desire to enjoy more, continue to serve with or without encouragement from people and situations around you. When the time comes, God will indeed bless you.

• Understand that you are not just on earth to occupy space but to make an impact. Let this desire be in you as a maid to make an impact and one of the ways to make an impact is by empowering others. This will equally help to speed up your promotion else, when there is none to do the job, you will be surprised that with grey hair, you will still be serving.

• Maids, also learn to see disappointment as God's appointment and by so doing, you will begin to understand its purpose. Remember always that hidden in some of your biggest disappointments are treasures of truth that literally transform your life and your future. Do not say because of past disappointments, you will no longer render the necessary support. Such action will hinder your spiritual growth by weakening your spiritual insight.

- If you are a fulltime employee in the church, support your master's vision financially, give more time above your paid hours and use your core gift in ensuring that his God given vision materialises.

- Understand that in other for you to be blessed, avoid focusing on reward but rather think daily on what you can give for the work of God.

Masters should also bear these in their hearts when dealing with their maids:

- A good master will always desire the progress of the maid but the bad master will only be concerned about himself and the job. If ninety nine per cent of some masters' calls is a request for a service to be rendered, this should be curtailed.

It should not only be when you want them to execute a task for you or verify if a task has been done that you will call else, it may get to a stage when your calls will be ignored. It is important also that you call and pray for your maids, ask about their welfare and discuss other issues that may not be work related.

- For a master to enjoy the service of his maid, ensure you do everything within your ability to ensure that the seed of greatness deposited by God in her life germinates.

- Never underestimate the role played by this group of people in your life. Never assume that they do not know what they want in life by being under you. You will be surprised that the after effect of such a thought will be beyond your comprehension. Naaman, as a leper, also got healed through the help of his own maid. She gave him the information that delivered him and cured him of his disease.

2 Kings 5:2, "And the Syrians had gone out on raids, and had brought back captive a young girl from the land of Israel. She waited on Naaman's wife. 3 Then she said to her mistress, "If only my master were with the prophet who is in Samaria! For he would heal him of his leprosy."

2 Kings 5:10 -15, "And Elisha sent a messenger to him, saying, "Go and wash in the Jordan seven times, and your flesh shall be restored to you, and you shall be clean." 11 But Naaman became furious, and went away and said, "Indeed, I said to myself, 'He will surely come out to me, and stand and call on the name of the LORD his God, and wave his hand over the place, and heal the leprosy.' 12 Are not the Abanah and the Pharpar, the rivers of Damascus, better than all the waters of Israel? Could I not wash in them and be clean?" So he turned and went away in a rage. 13 And his servants came near and spoke to him, and said, "My father, if the prophet had told you to do something great, would you not have done it? How much more then, when he says to you, 'Wash, and be clean'?" 14 So he went down and dipped seven times in the Jordan, according to the saying of the man of God; and his flesh was restored like the flesh of a little child, and he was clean. 15 And he returned to the man of God, he and all his aides, and came and stood before him; and he said, "Indeed, now I know that there is no God in all the earth, except in Israel; now therefore, please take a gift from your servant."

- Be an encourager, destiny navigator and a dream interpreter to them. Moreover, empower them to become self-reliant. This will enable them to be of help to others.
- Encourage your maids to pursue career in the ministry most especially those working fulltime. The bible says in *Matthew 9:37-38"37 Then He said to His disciples, "The harvest truly is plentiful, but the labourers are few. 38Therefore pray the Lord of the harvest to send out labourers into His harvest."*

  They could become church planters; counsellors, etc. Some people say that ministerial work is not a career but the call of God. Whichever way we understand this, whatever one does on daily basis and earns his or her livelihood from is a profession and this is not different from the meaning of career. Masters encourage your maids to make the work of the ministry a profession just as Apostle Peter gave up his fishing business and became a fisher of men. These maids are already in the boat with you, they have higher knowledge and understanding of the work in the ministry than those working part time or voluntary basis.

- Also, it is of necessity that a wise master sets a date for the exit of his servant the very first day the servant or helper came into his life. Have a settlement plan for someone that has served you for a particular period of time. This will help others also to come in and serve. A master should not keep a maid in a particular position for a long time or plan that she will be there for life. This is against God's plan and purpose for man. God has not created any man to be static but rather dynamic. He has placed the desire in every one of us to have dominion. This is a desire for progress and to get to the top. The top is not only meant for a particular group of people. Every child of God is meant for the top.

Genesis 1:26-28, "Then God said, "Let Us make man in Our image, according to Our likeness; let them have dominion over the fish of the sea, over the birds of the air, and over the cattle, over all the earth and over every creeping thing that creeps on the earth." 27 So God created man in His own image; in the image of God He created him; male and female He created them. 28 Then God blessed them, and God said to them, "Be fruitful and multiply; fill the earth and subdue it; have dominion over the fish of the sea, over the birds of the air, and over every living thing that moves on the earth."

Regardless of the present circumstance of the maid, this does not mean that this is the concluding chapter. It is an action being carried out in the process of time. Therefore it will be wrong for any master to assume that a particular servant will remain with him for life. If a master has such assumption, it is ungodly and against biblical injunction for the creation of man. Even if the person remains for life, there should be a change in the person's title, role and responsibilities.

- Good maids also carry blessings. Masters can equally enjoy prosperity beyond measure by reason of God's grace in the life of the maid or servant. His business and ministry will flourish beyond measure during the period of her service. It is important that masters should be able to discern and appreciate such grace upon the life of such maid. When Joseph entered Potiphar's house, he brought great blessings with him and when he went to Pharoah's palace, the entire nation prospered. When Jacob was about to return home to his own family, Laban, his father-in-law, said he should stay with him because he has learned by experience that the Lord has blessed him for the sake of Jacob.

- In case a master plays dual role both as a shepherd and a boss, it is very important you learn the skills on how to combine these roles very well in order not to sin against God and man. It could be tough but with the help of the Holy Spirit, wisdom and knowledge will be made sufficient for you in Jesus name; Amen. My suggestion is that masters who play dual role should first of all play the role of a shepherd before the role of a boss. When you prioritise your role and put the shepherd role first, it will be very easy to play the role of a boss. It becomes effortless. As a shepherd, you are required to care for your sheep and there is no sheep that enjoys the care of the shepherd that will eagerly want to leave the presence of the shepherd. A sheep that enjoys the care of the shepherd will not want to see the shepherd unhappy for any reason. That sheep knows what to do and at the right time too. But if you put the role of the boss first before the shepherd, you will be surprised that every activity and relationship end on that level. You may think as a shepherd that your servants are following you, but it is a mistake. If you look back by chance or reflection, you will realise that they are no longer following you but looking for an alternative shepherd that can fill that position in their lives. Masters that play dual role should be first a genuine shepherd before being a boss. This is also seen in the way you counsel your servant. If I may ask, do you put the interest of the job first or what God says concerning such issues? Do you know that when you put the interest of the job first, the servant knows where you are heading to? This action will cause the servant to seek counsel elsewhere and thereby limiting the level of information you know about such a servant. This destroys good relationship; therefore masters should apply godly wisdom and caution.

- Masters should never allow any set up or gang up to frustrate the works of their servants all in a bid to give others room or opportunity to grow and develop. Proper channel of communication should be followed when trying to groom others.

This will ensure that your servants are not side-tracked but have a clear understanding of what is going on. It is wrong for a master to assume that because a servant will not support the idea, therefore should not be involved from the beginning. Whether as a master you receive support or not, it is important you communicate. This makes the servant feel relevant. It will not be proper that until when issues go the wrong way before you bring it to the notice of your maids and thereby requesting for ideas on how they could be resolved. This is unwise. It encourages strife rather than love and peace.

- Remember always that they are humans made in God's image and likeness and not robots. Treat them with love and respect.

- Masters, remember always that maids on godly mission are very few. They may not possess everything you desire in a servant but there are rare good qualities that they may have and more importantly is the fear of God. Kindly assist them to pursue and acquire other things that they may not have, for example, a good education. Masters should not tolerate mediocrity but encourage them to develop themselves by being supportive.

Wisdom Pill: You cannot see a woman that speaks posh English and make her to suddenly replace the mother that gave birth to you because she comes from a remote village. Moreover, you cannot kill your mother because she is poor and replace her with a wealthy mother.

- Masters, should kindly help to preserve the passion of the maids for the job. Avoid doing anything that will destroy such passion. Encourage them in every way and make them a high flyer.

- The master that belong to the category of destiny mothering (nurturing) and not destiny murdering (wasting) should not give up. Continue to build the destiny of people serving under you and mentor them very well and as such be rest assured that the future is full of good harvest. A man that trains a woman has trained a generation. So also, a master that lifts the hand of the maid has lifted a generation. You that lift the hand of your maid spiritually, financially, academically, materially will enjoy the harvest of the seeds sown. Even if the maid turns out to be ungrateful, do not give up for you will reap what you have sown. Masters, never relent in doing good.

There are also suggestions to the master's wives to bear in mind:

- Encourage and support your husbands' vision by praying for your husband's maids. They are equally yours as well.
- Never see them as rivals or become envious of their position. When you start developing such feeling, you are creating room for the devil to begin his manipulations.
- Avoid listening to gossips that will frustrate their services and jeopardise the good relationship you may have with them.
- Be a good friend, sister and mother to them. They will ensure they preserve that which is yours in your absence and not destroy it.

- People may not flock around you because of your position as the master's wife; this may lead to some feelings of loneliness so also are maids. Maids that are very close to their masters find themselves in such state. People do not also flock around them because of the nature of their job and thereby finding themselves in lonely state amidst crowd. You will realise that both of you are of the same father and ought to be very close friends, encouraging and supporting each other.

For those planning to become a maid in God's vineyard, it is a good thought but, re-examine your motives.

- Are you interested in serving in other for you to have access to the master and thereby destroying his vision?
- Are you interested in the work because of the financial and material gains?
- Are you interested because you want to assist in the fulfilment of his vision?

  Your motive is very important. Just as marriage is, so also is this service. For a marriage to be successful, a wise girl would not go into marriage because of what she is going to gain but what she is going to give. Marriage is not about what you get out of it but what you give to it. Therefore, you must be ready to make sacrifices in other for you to succeed on this journey just as Ruth made a sacrifice by leaving her comfort zone and followed Naomi in the book of Ruth 1:6-16,*"Then she arose with her daughters-in-law that she might return from the country of Moab, for she had heard in the country of Moab that the LORD had visited His people by giving them bread. ⁷ Therefore she went out from the place where she was, and her two daughters-in-law with her; and they went on the way to return to the land of Judah. ⁸ And Naomi said to her two daughters-in-law, "Go, return each to her mother's house. The LORD deal kindly with you, as you have dealt with the dead and with me. ⁹ The LORD grant that you may find rest, each in the house of her husband." So she kissed them, and they lifted up their voices and wept. ¹⁰ And they said to her, "Surely we will return with you to your people." ¹¹ But Naomi said, "Turn back, my daughters; why will you go with me? Are there still sons in my womb, that they may be your husbands? 12 Turn back, my daughters, go — for I am too old to have a husband. If I should say I have hope, if I should have a husband tonight and should also bear sons, 13 would you wait for them till they were grown? Would you restrain yourselves from having husbands? No, my daughters; for it grieves me very much for your sakes that the hand of the LORD has gone out against me!" 14 Then they lifted up their voices and wept again; and Orpah kissed her mother-in-law, but Ruth clung to her. 15 And she said, "Look, your sister-in-law has gone back to her people and to her gods; return after your sister-in-law." 16 But Ruth said: "Entreat me not to leave you, or to turn back from following after you; for wherever you go, I will go; and wherever you lodge, I will lodge; your people shall be my people, and your God, my God.*

Orpah was not prepared to sacrifice anything. I believe she wanted to follow Naomi because Ruth made similar decision but eventually went back but Ruth was determined and prepared to go with Naomi. Her mind was made up. She never thought of what the outcome will be and possibly her destiny as some will think today. She just wanted to follow Naomi. An intending maid should be ready to make sacrifices in other to ensure her master's vision is fulfilled. If you are not ready to do this, please do not bother to venture into it for it will amount to an absolute waste of time because you may not get to your place of fulfilment.

On a final note, maids should bear in mind that there is no perfect master for as long as we are still in the flesh, we all have our weaknesses. If you are looking for a perfect master before you can serve in the vineyard of God, you will never find one till eternity comes. The only perfect master is our Lord Jesus Christ. Therefore, let your services be rendered unto Him and not man and by so doing, you will not be disappointed. Execute your service as if Christ is standing by and watching you because on the day of judgement, all secrets will be revealed and I pray you will not be found wanting in Jesus name, Amen.

Masters love your maids. Maids love your masters.

Note: If you have been blessed by this book, please kindly forward your comments to this email address: sistersheart24@gmail.com or on my Facebook: Ruth Omoregie. I will appreciate your comments.

God bless you!